Adrift

For my friend mentor
+ the who make it
possible —

MR. JOHN LAZARUS —

MARCUS YOUSSEF

Adrift

From the novel
Adrift on the Nile, by Naguib Mahfouz

Talonbooks

Talonbooks
P.O. Box 2076, Vancouver, British Columbia, Canada V6B 3S3
www.talonbooks.com

Typeset in Méridien and Frutiger and printed and bound in Canada.

First Printing: 2008

The publisher gratefully acknowledges the financial support of the
Canada Council for the Arts; the Government of Canada through the
Book Publishing Industry Development Program; and the Province of
British Columbia through the British Columbia Arts Council and the
Book Publishing Tax Credit for our publishing activities.

Library and Archives Canada Cataloguing in Publication

Youssef, Marcus
        Adrift / Marcus Youssef.

A play.
ISBN 978-0-88922-585-5

        1. Egypt—Social life and customs—21st century—Drama.
        I. Title.
PS8597.O89A78 2008   C812'.54   C2008-901057-4

For my father, George
My brother, Camyar
And his father, Cyrus

Adrift was first produced as *Adrift on the Nile* at the LSPU Hall, St. John's, Newfoundland, as part of the 2006 Magnetic North Theatre Festival. This first script was commissioned by neworld theatre and the Magnetic North Theatre Festival, and developed in association with the Playwrights Theatre Centre, Vancouver. It was co-written by Marcus Youssef and Camyar Chai.

The play was then rewritten by Marcus Youssef and presented by the Vancouver East Cultural Centre, at the Cultch, in February 2007. The text that follows is from this production.

Both productions were directed by Camyar Chai.

In St. John's:

Cast

Alex Lazaridis Ferguson	ANIS
James Fagan Tait	AMM
Kathleen Duborg	LAYLA
James Long	MUSTAFA
Laara Sadiq	SANIYA
Marcus Youssef	ALI
Bill Marchant	RAGAB
Adrienne Wong	SENA
Maiko Bae Yamamoto	SAMARA
Sam Shalabi	MUSICIAN

Design Team

Sam Shalabi	Original Score
Mara Gottler	Costumes
Rob Lewis	Set and Properties
Jonathan Ryder	Lighting
Tim Matheson	Projections

Production Team

Adrienne Wong	Producer
Jessica Chambers	Stage Manager
Anne Taylor	Production Manager
Jonathan Ryder	Technical Director
Martin Kinch	Dramaturge
Liliane Karnouk	Cultural Consultant
Sumayya Kassamali	Research & Production Assistant
Sydney Cavanaugh	Costume Assistant
Kevin MacDuff	Crew

In Vancouver, there were the following changes and additions:

Tom Pickett	AMM
Tom McBeath	ALI
Francesca Granzini	Costume Designer
Anne Taylor	Stage Manager
Danielle Fecko	Apprentice Stage Manager
Justine Fafard	Production Manager
Guillermo Verdecchia	Additional Dramaturgy
Amos Hertzman	Sound Engineer

Special Thanks

Mary Vingoe and Magnetic North, Duncan Low, Heather Redfern and the VECC, Richard Prokopanko and the Alcan Performing Arts Award, the board and staff of neworld theatre, the many arts councils that supported this show, Amanda Fritzlan, Zak and Oscar Youssef, John Murphy, Mara Coward, the Hern-Coutures, the Bolkhen-Herns, the Hutchison-Poyntzs and the Johnstons.

Setting

A Nile River houseboat, in downtown Cairo. April 2007.

Characters

ANIS, auditor in the Ministry of Health

MUSTAFA, commercial lawyer

LAYLA, copy writer in the Ministry of Foreign Affairs

ALI, editor of a weekly news magazine, and a Coptic
Christian

SANIYA, wife of a rich developer

RAGAB, film actor

*All of the above are in their late thirties to early forties, and have
been friends since university.*

AMM ABDUH, Nubian from the Aswan region, servant to
whoever rents the houseboat

SAMARA, freelance journalist, in her twenties

One.

ANIS. Looking at the audience.

ANIS

You ready? Good. I'm glad you are.

What do you think of when someone says Egypt, the Middle East? Pyramids and car bombs? Fanatics and burkhas? Aladdin? Born in Arizona, moved to Babylonia?

Or me. Little old me. Getting really stoned.

Music. He tokes.

So, about three weeks ago I was at work, in the Mogamma Building, in downtown Cairo. It's so fucking ugly, this building. Sorry. Anyway, I was at my desk, doing what I usually do, watching a cockroach climb the wall, and I look up and outside my window I see this giant whale. Bit of a shock, when you're on the fourteenth floor. Then the whale floats over and starts tapping on the glass with its fin. I opened the window. What are you going to do? "I've been watching you," the whale tells me. "If I were you, I'd just end it all right now. The window's open. Go on." A whale with keen psychological insight. I was going to ask him some questions: you know, "Do you have some kind of degree? And, what's with the flying?" But right then, my boss barges in and he's really pissed. Apparently I gave him a report on wait-list times and, well, it was blank. Guess I forgot to save. Whoops. "How can you type out a whole thirty page report and forget to save the file?" my boss wants to know. Good question. I was going to refer it to the whale, but by then it had split. "I know exactly how," my boss tells me. "Because you were stoned!"

ANIS tokes.

Aw, come on! Stoned? Me? At work? What are you talking about? I don't smoke dope, marijuana, kif. It's bad for you. It dulls your senses, blocks out the world and MAKES YOU FORGET; who would want to do that, when the icecaps are melting and there's troops on the streets and and world's going to hell in a hand basket and what are you doing? Well, twenty-eight thousand keystrokes of data entry, if you're asking me.

Seen any airborne whales lately? Could be a global phenomenon. Maybe they're adapting. Maybe there's nothing left for them in the sea.

Cairo. You. Me. April, month of dust and lies.

The whale was right. Three weeks ago, all I really wanted was to die.

ANIS sings "Baby Beluga."

Two.

Party's on. LAYLA, MUSTAFA are into it. ALI's there, too.
RAGAB is sound asleep.

LAYLA

Anis, there's no whales in the Nile River. There can't be.
It's fresh water.

ALI

He's just joking.

RAGAB snores.

LAYLA

You're lacing your coffee in the morning and you're
smoking at night, every night, even when we don't come.

ANIS

Especially when you don't come.

LAYLA

You can't keep this up forever.

MUSTAFA hangs up his phone.

MUSTAFA

Can't keep up much, from what I hear. Guess who just
called? You know that American powdered milk I got my
hands on, because nobody in Darfur could digest it? I just
sold it to a Venezuelan NGO. The Venezuelans are going to
donate it to destitute families in the States. To make the

American government look bad. Hilarious. You should do a story, Ali. How Egyptians survive by selling Americans their own milk.

ALI

Cairo Now's more about good-news stories.

MUSTAFA

Right. "*Cairo Now*." I don't know about that magazine of yours. That whole multifaith, can't-we-all-just-get-along thing is more like *Cairo About Twenty-Five Years Ago*.

ALI

Somebody has to try to elevate the level of the debate. It's a losing battle but—

ANIS

The Faith.

ALI

What about it?

ANIS

That's the paper people read. *The Faith*.

MUSTAFA

He's right. That jihadist rag's got a circulation of about 800 million.

ANIS

There's copies all over my office.

ALI

When people get scared, they go to the lowest common denominator.

ANIS

Sheikh Ahmad's in *The Faith*.

LAYLA

Fuck Sheikh Ahmad. He's a lunatic.

ANIS

Today he said that Egypt's Christians are the enemy within.

ALI

Jesus.

MUSTAFA

Exactly.

LAYLA

Can we not talk about that muckraking hack?

ANIS

We're all going to hell.

ALI

Ah, well. What can you do? Jihad sells.

MUSTAFA

But you're a Christian.

ALI

People like the drama, that's all. I may be a Christian, but as a publisher, in business terms, I get it.

MUSTAFA

Better be careful, crucifix boy, one of these days Ahmad and his thugs might just come looking for your head.

LAYLA

OK, that's enough.

MUSTAFA

Sorry, baby. A joke. You know, the weird kind, that's sort of real.

LAYLA

Sleeping with you was the biggest mistake I ever made.

MUSTAFA

Think you'll make it again?

LAYLA

History does seem to repeat itself.

MUSTAFA

I'll be America, you be Iraq.

ALI

Shock and awe. Kaboom.

RAGAB snores.

What's with Ragab?

MUSTAFA

He's been partying all week. Turn up the music! Look at me, I'm gonna dance like the whale!

ANIS

Amm!

Shift. The others fade away. AMM enters.

AMM

This place is a sty.

ANIS

Where have you been?

AMM

Watching TV. Mike from Sacramento just went all in. *World Championship of Poker*. And there was a car bomb in a Baghdad market. One hundred and twelve dead.

(*indicating RAGAB*)

Your friend the movie star bought me a satellite. Which was nice.

But he'll still have to face God's judgement.

ANIS

How do you think he'll do?

AMM shakes his head.

What do you know about judgement?

AMM

Nothing. It isn't possible for me to imagine it.

ANIS

Bullshit. You think God is some big black guy who wanders around bringing people down when they're trying to get high.

AMM

Do you want more hashish?

ANIS

Yes.

AMM

The police are watching my dealer.

ANIS

Relax. It's all good.

AMM

You smoke too much.

ANIS

Maybe I smoke just the right amount.

AMM

You need to get rid of your friends.

ANIS

Why?

AMM

So you can face it. You're being swallowed.

ANIS

Do you see the whale?

AMM

May God have mercy on you.

ANIS

No, no no no, please. Enough with God.

AMM

Fine.

ANIS

(*to audience*) Amm Abduh, our servant. A peasant, a
Nubian, from near the Aswan Dam. That explained his
fondness for religion. Only peasants waste time thinking
about God and what happens when we die. Which'll be
about a second from now, relatively speaking.

The whale was outside the boat.

The whale's jaws open.

Talking. Saying, "You're alive for what? Seventy, eighty years?"

Actually, here in Egypt, life expectancy's more like sixty. Better than Zambia. There it's thirty.

"How long are you going to be dead? You hate this boat, the world, your so-called friends. Go on, get it over with. I'm a whale. You're Jonah. Be brave. Jump."

ANIS considers. RAGAB snores.

He snaps his fingers. Switch to a different room.

SANIYA and LAYLA.

SANIYA

So I hear this weird noise, and I go to open …

She stops.

Sorry.

Digs in her purse. Produces her cell.

Khalid. He's calling every five minutes.

Opens the cell.

I told you, I'm at my sister's. I don't know. I'm very angry. Goodbye.

Closes the cell, puts it away.

Says he's counting the hours till I come back. Prick.

Anyway, when I walk in, there's Khalid with that awful big-thighed woman from the seventh floor and he's all hunched over. Oh, I won't even tell you what he likes to do. Anyway, he's doing it to her and apparently she's enjoying it. Grotesque. After all his complaining about me coming to the houseboat. They're all the same.

LAYLA

Your dear husband's a little more the same than most.

SANIYA
You were the smart one, Layla.

LAYLA
What do you mean?

SANIYA
Foreign Affairs, it's so glamorous.

LAYLA
You're right. The Ministry's glass ceiling is pretty fantastic.

SANIYA
What does it matter? The important thing is we're all here,
together.

LAYLA
Can I ask a favour?

SANIYA
Sure.

LAYLA
I know, I'm sorry.

SANIYA
How much?

LAYLA
A hundred. Two, if you can manage it. Things are pretty
tight.

SANIYA
Right.

LAYLA
I don't know what else to do.

SANIYA

It's fine.

LAYLA

My boss.

SANIYA

I know.

LAYLA

I'm appealing.

SANIYA

I don't have any cash. I have to go to the bank.

LAYLA

Great.

SANIYA

Tomorrow.

LAYLA

Thanks. God-freak boss told me that he thought I should cover my face.

Back with ANIS. RAGAB snores. ANIS pretends to have a conversation with him.

ANIS

—So, Ragab, how was the glamorous premiere of your big new movie, *Night of the Scarab*? Is it really about an Egyptian Secret Service agent who saves the world from an alien invasion funded by Israel? I was hoping that you would invite me. You know, because I don't get out much.

—I did invite you. I left a message with Amm. You didn't get it?

—Typical. You can't trust a Black African.

—Now, now, Anis. Everyone's human, even the Blacks of
Africa.

*SANIYA tiptoes in, with LAYLA behind. She waves, mouthing,
"Hi Anis!" and then puts her finger to her lips.*

SANIYA
Sshhh!

She points behind her. MUSTAFA enters, covering ALI's eyes.

ALI
Why are you subjecting me—

MUSTAFA
Ta-da.

ALI
Oh my God.

SANIYA
Saniya, actually, but you can call me God if you like. Or
Goddess, God willing.

ALI
Two-and-a-half months. No messages, no calls.

SANIYA
Oh, sweetheart, I'm sorry. You know what he's like. This
time, I'm not going back. I promise. Kiss?

ALI
Good thing I'm such a pushover.

SANIYA
It's what I love about you.

ALI

Who'd have thought I'd end up being the one hanging
around pining for you?

SANIYA

I missed you so much. Finally we're all together.

MUSTAFA

Mm. Hey, baby, what's shakin'?

LAYLA

Ah, the burden of history.

Sorry.

She pulls out a cell.

LAYLA

Hello? Oh, hi.

LAYLA steps out. MUSTAFA pursues. ALI and SANIYA snuggle.

ANIS

What about me?

ALI

You're our Master of Ceremonies. The keeper of our
hearth.

LAYLA

(*on the cell*) OK. Yes, Sir.

ALI

Can't have you distracted by base earthly desires.

ANIS

Ha ha ha.

LAYLA
  (*on the cell*) Fine.

ALI
  You could always give Ragab a feel.

ANIS
  I'd rather have a flaming thornbrush shoved up my ass.

  LAYLA hangs up the phone.

LAYLA
  Shit.

MUSTAFA
  What?

LAYLA
  Nothing.

ANIS
  (*to audience*) And then, finally, something happened.

  SAMARA.

SAMARA
  Hey, Ali.

  Lights out.

ANIS
  Amm!

  AMM lights SAMARA, who is frozen.
  ANIS goes to her. Examines her, like a statue.

  Who is she?

AMM
  I don't know.

ANIS
You just let her walk in?

AMM
I was watching TV.

ANIS
(*to audience*) She reminded me of ...

AMM
Cleopatra.

> *Back to normal.* LAYLA *rifles through her work bag.*

ANIS
Hello.

SAMARA
Sorry. I didn't mean to startle you.

ALI
Samara. This is a surprise.

ANIS
I've been wanting ... to be startled.

MUSTAFA
Hey, Nubia-boy, you get paid to keep people out.

AMM
Arnold Schwarzenegger just bought the first bio-diesel Hummer.

MUSTAFA
Great, you're fired.

AMM

And the Sahara Desert has spread into Europe. A fifth of Spain is now a desert.

ALI

Just go back to your hut. Everyone, this is Samara.

ALI indicates to ANIS to put away the pipe. ANIS does weird mime back.

MUSTAFA

Look, I was just about to get hot and heavy with my ex here. I've been working on her all night.

During the following, LAYLA starts scribbling notes for work.

ALI

We ran into each other at an opening last week. God-awful thing.

SAMARA

Ali invited me to drop by.

MUSTAFA

Nice. Never mentioned it to us.

ALI

Samara's contributing to *Cairo Now*. Very promising young writer.

SAMARA

Thank you. I hope this isn't a bad time.

RAGAB wakes up, disoriented.

ALI

No, no. This is Saniya.

SANIYA barely acknowledges her.

She just got here, too.

ANIS

Please. Uh. Make yourself. At home.

SAMARA

If you're busy, no big deal.

ANIS

Do you want a drink? I mean, not a drink. If you want. You don't drink?

SAMARA

No.

At a loss, ANIS offers her the pipe.

RAGAB

Hi. Look, I meant to come back to the party.

SAMARA

Excuse me?

RAGAB

I just got sucked in by my friends, here; I was going to come get you, I must have fallen asleep—

SAMARA

I'm not sure I understand.

RAGAB

The Bel Air tent. At the *Scarab* premiere after-party. You're … in continuity … makeup. No, a PA. Best boy. I remember. But you weren't wearing that scarf.

SAMARA

I think you're confusing me with someone else.

RAGAB
I am? Right. I'm sorry. It's been quite a week. I'm an actor.
I'm in a little film that just opened.

SAMARA
Night of the Scarab?

RAGAB
You've heard of it?

SAMARA
Yeah. Biggest opening weekend in Cairo history.

RAGAB
Is that right?

SAMARA
It's always interesting when an action movie pretends to
be social commentary.

MUSTAFA
He's been boozing and whoring for days.

SAMARA
Mustafa, right?

MUSTAFA
Nice to meet you.

SAMARA
Ali warned me about you.

MUSTAFA
What'd he say?

SAMARA
I think it was off the record.

ANIS

Obnoxious prick.

SAMARA

Not exactly.

ALI

But that was the general sense. I said the first thing that came into my head.

MUSTAFA

We Muslims have long memories, crucifix boy.

(*to SAMARA*) So is the headdress just a fashion statement or are you really worried we're going to get turned on by your hair?

SAMARA

Wow. I don't know what to say. I do have pretty nice hair.

SANIYA

Excuse us.

> *SANIYA and ALI leave. LAYLA continues to work. AMM enters, to clean.*

RAGAB

Here. Please sit down. Relax.

SAMARA

You sure it's OK?

RAGAB

Of course.

MUSTAFA

What?

LAYLA

My boss. Now I have to draft a response to Bush saying that democracy is spreading through the Middle East.

MUSTAFA

So, I'm out?

LAYLA

Sorry, toots.

AMM leaves.

SAMARA

Is he a Nubian?

RAGAB

Uh, no, I don't think so.

ANIS

Yes.

RAGAB

Yes. He kind of came with the place. We were going to let him go, but, well, you know. I think it's really important to be kind to the less fortunate.

SAMARA

Most people don't remember that we wiped out their ancestral lands.

RAGAB

We did?

ANIS

In the '60s. When we built the Aswan Dam.

RAGAB

Oh, right. The Dam.

ANIS
It was the flooding. It forced the Nubians to migrate north.

SAMARA
Where they became our servants.

RAGAB
Of course he's also the prayer leader at the mosque next door.

MUSTAFA
And a pimp.

RAGAB
Light the pipe, would ya?

MUSTAFA
Yes, massa; right away, massa.

RAGAB
So, Omar was on set today.

LAYLA
Uh-oh.

LAYLA and MUSTAFA get up.

RAGAB
Where are you going?

LAYLA
Omar story.

SAMARA
Omar?

RAGAB
Omar Sharif.

MUSTAFA

Heard this one about eighteen times.

RAGAB

But it happened today.

LAYLA

It happens every day. If he's still talking in fifteen minutes, put your scarf on, Anis, and sneak out the back.

They leave.

RAGAB

Omar gets a "cameo" in everything. Because he was "Dr. Zhivago." When he shows up today, he doesn't even know his lines. Seriously. I mean he's a nice guy and everything, but you just want to grab him by his little cashmere suit and say, "You know, just 'cause you half made it in Hollywood, that doesn't mean you're the only Egyptian actor that ever lived." You can't though, because of course he's smoked eighteen packs of cigarettes a day for four thousand years. You so much as touch him, and the tumour'll burst through his chest.

RAGAB and the pipe.

Don't mind them. They've got "opinions" about everything.

SAMARA

Opinions are all good.

RAGAB

You're pretty "political."

SAMARA

Yes.

RAGAB
    And devout.

SAMARA
    More or less. I mean, I wasn't always. My parents are
    secular.

    Cell. RAGAB pulls it out.

RAGAB
    Sorry. Keep talking. (*on the phone*) Hello? Hey.
    (*to ANIS*) Anis!

    *He gestures at ANIS to play host, and ducks aside to talk on the
    phone.*

ANIS
    Uh ... you want a ... glass of water?

SAMARA
    I'm good.

ANIS
    Smart. It's very polluted.

SAMARA
    You don't get it from the Nile, do you?

ANIS
    I don't know where Amm gets anything. Crazy Africans.

SAMARA
    Egypt's in Africa.

ANIS
    That's true.

SAMARA

Do you know how the Minister of Water Quality got his job?

ANIS

Uh, no.

SAMARA

He's married to President Mubarak's sister. His only management experience was as Honorary Chair of the Cairo Horse Show.

ANIS

That's crazy.

Pause.

Did you know that President Mubarak's sister is actually a man in drag?

SAMARA

What?

ANIS

Sorry. A joke. Not funny. I haven't been feeling very good.

SAMARA

Are you sick?

RAGAB hangs up his cell.

RAGAB

My apologies. Production Assistant. Movies are a crazy business. Look, I have to go. But I want you to promise to come back tomorrow.

SAMARA

Are you sure it's OK?

RAGAB

I pay for all this. Right, Anis?

Walk me out, I'll show you the garden.

SAMARA is hesitant.

Come join us, Anis.

(to *SAMARA, on their way out*) You know, I've actually been thinking about becoming more observant.

On their way out.

ANIS

Wait.

He tries to get up.

Hang on.

His back. Too much.

I'll be right there.

Shift. ANIS with the audience.

Love at first sight. A hoary cliché. As bad as car bombs and shifty-eyed fanatics. That's the weird thing about clichés, though: they can't be clichés unless in some way they're true. That's a cliché, too. About clichés. Ha.

It wasn't Cleopatra she reminded me of.

It was our little village. Three hundred kilometres and about four lifetimes from here.

And our wedding night, when I first touched my wife's hair.

The next night she came early.

Three.

The next night. SAMARA.

SAMARA
Hey.

ANIS
Hi.

She goes into her purse.

SAMARA
Excuse me.

She pulls out her BlackBerry.

Hello?

No.

I told you. I know what he said.

Well, since he's so into you, maybe you should see what he's up to tonight.

She puts it away.

(*to ANIS*) Sorry about that. This guy.

Beautiful here.

Pause.

I saw a picture of President Mubarak's sister at the paper today. She does kind of look like a man in drag.

ANIS
    Told you.

SAMARA
    Are you originally from Cairo?

ANIS
    No.

SAMARA
    Where?

ANIS
    Little village. Up the delta.

SAMARA
    What made you leave?

ANIS
    Oh, no reason.

SAMARA
    I love those villages. Farmers and peasants, they're not all
    caught up in the crazy go go go. It's primitive, for sure, but
    in so many ways it seems more real. Don't you think?

ANIS
    You must be from the city.

SAMARA
    Yeah.

ANIS
    I was glad to get away from my village.

SAMARA
    Why?

        Pause. They speak at the same time.

SAMARA
What do you think's—

ANIS
You remind me of—

Sorry.

SAMARA
No, go ahead.

ANIS
No. After you.

SAMARA
I was just going to ask what you think's going to happen.

ANIS
Happen?

SAMARA
Two hundred thousand American troops in Iraq. Civil war
in Palestine. Israelis in Lebanon. Our so-called
"government." It's like the whole thing is teetering on the
brink.

ANIS
How old are you?

SAMARA
Twenty-five. Almost twenty-six.

ANIS
Right.

SAMARA

If we had a real election—God forbid—Muslim Brotherhood would win in a second. If they were allowed to run. What do you think of the Brotherhood?

ANIS

Not much.

SAMARA

Not much you don't think about them, or not much you don't like them.

ANIS

I can't remember.

SAMARA

You think politics is all bullshit.

ANIS

It is.

SAMARA

You know about the Nubians. How guys like Amm are basically our slaves.

ANIS

Knowing doesn't seem to make much difference.

SAMARA

It's something.

ANIS

The river under our feet is billions of years old.

SAMARA

Sorry?

ANIS

That starlight up there, it's travelled thousands of years to reach us at this very moment.

When you were nine or ten years old, another Bush fought a war against Iraq. Five hundred years before that was the crusades. Fifty years ago, it was the Nubians and the Dam. Now it's China's turn. Three Gorges Dam. What makes those work—cell phones, Blueberries, whatever you call them—it's a metal, called Coltan. You can only get it in the Congo, one of the poorest countries in the world. It fuelled a civil war, half a million dead children—over a rock. This century's rock. That's the thing. Nothing ever changes. This is what I talk about with the whale.

SAMARA

The whale?

ANIS

Yeah. But then, I don't get out much.

SAMARA

No, it's good. I've heard about the Coltan.

ANIS

What can you do? Basically the whole world uses a cell. I was just going to say that I'm glad you came.

RAGAB enters, on the cell.

RAGAB

Great. And sorry I didn't get back to you. I didn't lose your number. I just couldn't remember your name. Remember, Omar, spades are trump.

(*to SAMARA*) Hey.

SAMARA

Hi.

RAGAB

    Omar Sharif. He might drop by later. If he doesn't drop dead first. I ordered some Perrier.

    Amm, let's go!

    They go. AMM enters, carrying a large box of Perrier.

AMM

    Three hundred and twenty people dead from a heatwave in Southern France. Freak weather. For the seventh year in a row. And your friends are making a really big mess.

    Later. The party in mid-gear. ALI, ANIS, MUSTAFA, SAMARA, RAGAB, SANIYA, on her cell, and LAYLA, who is working.

MUSTAFA

    Come again. Boltan?

ANIS

    Coltan.

MUSTAFA

    (*doing a sci-fi voice*) Beware the Coltan.

SAMARA

    I'd completely forgotten about it. I remember skimming an essay a few years ago, but Anis reminded me. Half a million dead children in the Congo.

MUSTAFA

    So Saniya can pretend she's at her sister's in Maadi.

    SANIYA hangs up.

SANIYA

    Well, that's that.

ALI

    What'd you say?

SANIYA
That it's over.

ALI
Over?

SANIYA
Over.

ALI
Well, I won't say I'm disappointed.

SANIYA
He threatenened to freeze my account.

ALI
Don't worry about it, baby. We'll figure it out.

MUSTAFA
Ok, this stuff is definitely cut. Amm! The dope sucks!

A pot flies through the room.

LAYLA
You're right, Anis. We should try to do something for the
Coltan children. Though I don't have the faintest idea
what.

SAMARA
Start small. Write a letter.

MUSTAFA
To who? *Cairo Now*?

ALI
No one reads *Cairo Now*. How about President Bush?

ANIS

Don't be a jerk.

ALI

Dear Mr. Bush. We think the War on Terror is pretty cool.
We'd like you to declare a War on Coltan, as well.

MUSTAFA

And maybe a war on nightmares.

RAGAB

Not to mention a war on carbs.

MUSTAFA

I'd prefer crabs, actually. The little ones. I could really do
with a war on crabs.

LAYLA

Don't remind us.

SANIYA

What?

SAMARA

Nothing.

SANIYA

You look like you've just eaten a lemon. What?

SAMARA

Is Anis all right?

SANIYA

He's fine. Right, sweetie?

SAMARA

He doesn't look fine. He was being serious about the Coltan.

ALI

He's always been like that. Ever since I found him at Cairo U. Remember that? I was a prof. I taught all these monkeys. Before the purge.

I kept seeing him in the caf. He didn't look good, so I brought him back here. Mumbled something about being from a village outside Bani Suwayef. Real mess. I enrolled him in some classes. He did great, actually—smart kid. But he stopped going.

MUSTAFA

Had a good line on kif, though. A natural for Master of Ceremonies.

ALI

A friend of mine found him a job at the Ministry of Health.

SANIYA

God, it was twenty years ago. Can you believe it? You blink and it's gone.

SAMARA

I think that's what happens if you get too comfortable. At least if you're the kind of people who have everything they more or less want.

LAYLA

I don't quite understand. You think we have everything we want?

SAMARA

In material terms. You have a lot more than most people.

RAGAB

I think you're right. I think we have gotten too comfortable.

SAMARA

It's natural if all you think about is yourselves.

Pause. ANIS begins to look for something. Eventually, he will give up.

SANIYA

So, tell us about *The Faith*.

I had a look online. You write for them quite a bit.

SAMARA

That's true.

MUSTAFA

The Faith, eh? Nice.

RAGAB

What's *The Faith*?

SANIYA

Islamist weekly.

SAMARA

It pays.

ALI

Probably a lot better than *Cairo Now*.

LAYLA

Because it's funded by some extremist Saudi.

SAMARA

I think that kind of language is also pretty extreme.

MUSTAFA
 What about Sheikh Ahmad?

SAMARA
 What about George Bush?

LAYLA
 I'm dealing with him right now.

RAGAB
 Who's Sheikh Ahmad?

MUSTAFA
 Columnist.

ALI
 Hot-button type.

MUSTAFA
 He's got a thing for infidels.

LAYLA
 And beheading.

RAGAB
 Oh.

SAMARA
 He never actually said that.

ALI
 She's right.

LAYLA
 He implied it.

ALI

    He said when it comes to dealing with seditious apostates, sometimes the gloves have to come off. Or something like that.

SAMARA

    And the government used that as a pretext for shutting the whole paper down. For two weeks. They can torture engineers from the Brotherhood, but Sheikh Ahmad can't use a boxing metaphor.

    The Faith makes money. Do you know what they use the profits for?

    Running schools and hospitals in the slums. Because the government won't.

SANIYA

    Well, the government should.

SAMARA

    But they don't. They'd rather buy weapons.

MUSTAFA

    Maybe because they need them.

LAYLA

    Sadat got brutally assassinated by Islamic extremists, remember? Or is not politically correct to call them that?

MUSTAFA

    How about the Fuzzy Bunnies of Jihad?

SAMARA

    The Islamic Council's building a whole new housing tract in the City of the Dead.

SANIYA

    And when there's trouble, that's where it'll start.

SAMARA

Why do you think they'd want to make trouble? There's not a lot of nice houseboats in the City of the Dead.

SANIYA

You seem to be doing OK.

SAMARA

That's true. I'm like you. I have a BlackBerry, for God's sake. I just find that sometimes people make assumptions, if they don't have all the facts.

LAYLA

Ok, listen to this.

She reads from the notes she's been working on.

"In response to the American President's assertion that democracy is spreading through the Middle East, let us first say that the United States and Egypt are friends. And like all good friends, we must sometimes agree to disagree. And so let us be clear: Egypt and the United States are agreed on our unwavering commitment to agreement when we disagree."

What do you think?

MUSTAFA

It's fucking brilliant.

LAYLA

Thanks. Can somebody run me downtown? I'm going to glue it to my boss's desk.

AMM enters. The others fade.

AMM

Gerald Planter from Wichita. On *Deal or No Deal*. Top prize. A million dollars. Imagine what you could do with that.

ANIS

She's back again.

AMM

Who?

ANIS

The Imam chick.

AMM

She's been coming all week.

AMM hands him a book.

ANIS

Where did you find it?

AMM

In one of your old suitcases.

It's a book about the Prophet's daughter.

ANIS

Thanks for tracking it down.

AMM

Are you sure that's what she wants?

ANIS nervously plays with the book. Gets up. Walks.

SAMARA making notes on her BlackBerry.

ANIS

Hi.

SAMARA

You scared me.

SAMARA saves her notes and puts the BlackBerry away.

ANIS
    You can type on that?

SAMARA
    Yeah. It's basically a computer. Cool, huh?

ANIS
    What are you writing?

SAMARA
    Nothing. Some personal stuff.

ANIS
    I have something I wanted to—

        He goes to hand her the book. Cell.

SAMARA
    Sorry.

        She turns it off.

ANIS
    Who's that?

SAMARA
    This guy.

ANIS
    Your boyfriend.

SAMARA
    No. He works for my father. My parents are secular but
    they still think they should be able to choose my husband.
    Nice, huh?

ANIS

When did you start practising?

SAMARA

I was at U. Cairo. A bunch of us started going to mosque.
Experimenting, you know. After a while some of us
decided to try the scarf. Of course my parents freaked. But
they were stuck, right. Especially my mom. She's a VP at
Deloitte & Touche. Woman making decisions for herself,
right. Then Islamic Jihad bombed those tourists in Luxor.
That's when the government banned the headscarf on
campus.

ANIS

I remember that.

SAMARA

It was like, hang on. What are you all so afraid of? For the
first time in my life I feel like I'm actually part of
something that matters, and you're telling me I'm a
brainwashed terrorist.

ANIS

The book is called *Fatima is Fatima*. It's by Shariati. He's an
Iranian.

SAMARA

Yeah, yeah. Shariati, sure. He's a Shia, though.

ANIS

The person who gave it to me, she didn't believe in the
whole Sunni–Shia split.

SAMARA

I don't know about that.

ANIS

It's about the Prophet's daughter.

SAMARA

I know who Fatima is.

ANIS

Of course. It talks about her as an ideal for Muslim
women. Her strength, her courage, her willingness to fight.

It was a gift from a woman I knew. I want you to have it.

SAMARA

Thanks.

Why did you come to Cairo?

ANIS

We were farmers. My father had just died and the
government opened up the cotton market. Became way
cheaper to import it from the West.

SAMARA

Figures.

ANIS

And my wife and child died.

Pause.

SAMARA

At the same time?

ANIS

Yes.

SAMARA

How?

ANIS

Oh, you know.

SAMARA

No.

ANIS

Boring, really. A car, speeding through an intersection. Hit and run.

SAMARA

That sucks.

ANIS

You're more likely to get hit by a car.

SAMARA

Sorry?

ANIS

Than just about anything. Plane crash. Terrorist attack. Avian flu. It's in Egypt, now, eh? Chickens crossed the border from Gaza.

SAMARA

Did they catch the person who hit them?

ANIS

No. Never really tried, as far as I could tell.

SAMARA

Buried tragedy.

ANIS

What?

SAMARA
Nothing. Must have been so hard.

Pause.

Do you ever think about going somewhere, getting off this boat?

ANIS
I don't like to go out.

SAMARA
Might do you some good. There's lots of places. It's a big city. I could take you. We could go to the Hilton.

ANIS
And do what?

SAMARA
Have a coffee. Talk.

ANIS
I'd have to put on a suit.

SAMARA
Nah. The tea room's gotten pretty traditional.

ANIS
Maybe a shave.

SAMARA
That's true. You either go for the beard or you don't. The mid-way thing's a little confusing.

RAGAB appears, behind ANIS.

I should go.

ANIS
Already?

SAMARA

It's very late.

ANIS

If you stay long enough it starts to get early. Time's funny that way.

Look, I don't really talk about the accident. Much. So I'd appreciate you keeping it to yourself.

SAMARA

They know, though.

> *Pause.*

You never told them.

ANIS

It never came up.

> *Pause.*

SAMARA

It's not good to pretend, you know. Then everything stays the same.

ANIS

I certainly don't want it to do that.

SAMARA

Thanks for the book.

> *She leaves. ANIS alone, with the audience.*

ANIS

Look, Ma: no more whale.

> *AMM enters.*

AMM

Six–four in the seventh-inning stretch. Indians of Cleveland against the Braves of Atlanta. Sin Soo Choo, right-fielder from Korea. He hit a home-run in the sixth.

You like her.

ANIS

I loved her.

AMM

No. Cleopatra.

ANIS

Oh.

AMM

I've got a line on this stuff. Herbs. From the Sudan. They might help with your impotence.

ANIS

I'm not impotent.

AMM

That's not what the street girls say. They could make a difference. Expensive, though. Ten pounds now, twenty on delivery.

ANIS

They work?

AMM

That's what the Sudanese guy told me.

ANIS

All right.

AMM

Who knows? Maybe they'll make you into a man of steel.

(*leaving, he sings*)

Let me root, root, root for the home team,
If they don't win it's a shame.
For it's one, two, three strikes, you're out,
At the old ball game.

Four.

MUSTAFA's on his cell.

SANIYA

I don't see why you had to start some affirmative action program for faux-religious babes.

ALI

She's a good writer. On what I pay, the good ones don't usually stick around.

SANIYA

And she's gorgeous.

ALI

No.

SANIYA

She's not gorgeous? Are you telling me you'd be ogling her if she was old and fat? I was your student once, remember. I know how young women are when they get attracted to an authority figure.

ALI

I'm sixty years old, Saniya. I highly doubt she has any interest in me.

SANIYA

Sixty? When did you turn sixty?

ALI

Three weeks ago. You were back with your husband, remember.

ANIS

She's not faux.

RAGAB

Anis is right. I think she's very sincere.

LAYLA

How would you know?

RAGAB

We went for coffee last week. To the Hilton.

ANIS

Really?

RAGAB

She called me up out of the blue. Said she wanted to talk.

ANIS

About what?

RAGAB

How I feel about the movies I'm in, you know, blockbusters. And what it means to be in the public eye. It was cute. She's so serious. I took her to the studio, introduced her to a couple of producers. They were all terrified. Nothing freaks industry types out more than religion.

SANIYA

She's doing it to everybody. Yesterday she wanted to talk about when we were in university, my whole little poverty action thing. Wanted to know what had happened. I told her I do charity work now. And you may not consider the President's Council on Women an important forum, but it means something to me. I know the type. Fashion fundamentalist.

These kids, they grew up with everything, then they put a rag on their heads without the faintest idea what it means.

ALI
Sweetheart, relax.

SANIYA
Don't patronize me.

ALI
I'm not.

SANIYA
They don't know what we went through to get a little freedom in this country.

LAYLA
Can I talk to you for a second?

MUSTAFA
OK, so get this. That was US Army Procurement. In a couple of months, American soldiers in Iraq are gonna be taking dumps in genuine Egyptian-made latrines. I just sold 5,800 port-a-potties at 750 pounds a pop. It's part of a little economic development program for America's friends in the Arab world. Kind of makes you proud, huh?

AMM
(*from his hut*) Hugo Chavez just appointed himself President for Life. And a new show! A new show! *Armed and Famous*! Gary Coleman is learning how to shoot with an Uzi!

MUSTAFA

Me, I like to put my faith in things that I can sell.

RAGAB and ANIS.

RAGAB

So there's talk about a big epic thing, a film about the Suez War.

ANIS

Really?

RAGAB

You know, our one great victory. Standing up to the imperialists, masters of our own destiny. They want me to play General Nasser.

ANIS

Congratulations.

RAGAB

Yeah. I mean, I'm not really into politics but it's flattering. Nasser was the Arab world's greatest modern leader. Look, I've been meaning to talk to you.

ANIS

You are.

RAGAB

I just wanted to check in. I'm sorry if we haven't always been as supportive as we should.

ANIS

About what?

RAGAB

Nothing. It's great. It's just—it's good to see you coming out of your shell. And you never know. She might have a

thing for taking care of people. Religious girls can be like
that.

*Later. SAMARA, with LAYLA and SANIYA, who are really
stoned.*

LAYLA

She always promises to lend me money. Isn't that right,
Anis?

ANIS

Sure.

SANIYA

Oh, God, don't start.

LAYLA

I asked you three days ago.

SANIYA

I told you. He transferred the money out of my account.
Layla's always broke because she thinks it's so important
to take all these stands. Her boss is one of yours.

SAMARA

Mine?

SANIYA

You know.

SAMARA

No.

LAYLA

An Islamist.

SAMARA

That's a total generalization.

SANIYA

She calls him Jimmy Jihad.

LAYLA

They appointed him in February, after the demonstrations
got out of hand. Two weeks after he starts, out of nowhere
he bumps me down a pay bracket. Because of my
"provocative demeanour." Provocative demeanour. Please.
I told him, "I have a Masters from the University of
Jordan, Sir, and I'll be damned if anyone's going to tell me
what to wear." Really smart. Next day, he bumped me
down again. For failure to fulfill my duties. I could barely
live on what I made to begin with.

SANIYA

Why don't you talk to Ragab?

LAYLA

Fuck that. No.

SANIYA

You always ask me.

LAYLA

I never slept with you.

SAMARA

Aren't they your friends?

LAYLA

I'm a civil servant in the Ministry of Foreign Affairs. I can
take care of myself.

(*to SANIYA*) It's just for a few weeks, until my appeal goes
through. The tribunal's going to meet … eventually.

SANIYA

(*to LAYLA*) Come by tomorrow. I'll see what I can do.

LAYLA
    Thanks.

SANIYA
    (*to SAMARA*) Can I see your hair? Do you mind?

    She goes to her. Touches her hijab. Exposes a tiny bit of her hair.

    Mmm. So beautiful. And young, eh Layla? Remember
    when we turned heads like this one? You don't need this
    thing, you know. I mean, it's your choice, but hair that nice
    deserves to be seen. You should show it with pride.

SAMARA
    It's just hair. And, I don't know, I don't want to speak for
    anyone else but, for me, it actually makes things easier.

SANIYA
    You're shy.

SAMARA
    No, I expect to be taken seriously. Which is actually what I
    find happens. It's interesting, when you make the decision
    not to be an object, how suddenly people treat you
    differently.

SANIYA
    It is trendy. I guess all that stuff we used to worry about
    isn't cool anymore. You know, like equality. Making our
    own choices.

ANIS
    In the '60s women were forced to remove their scarves.

SANIYA
    Because in the villages they were totally controlled by
    men.

SAMARA

How can you speak for women in the villages?

LAYLA

How can you? My God, do you have any idea what you're talking about? You grew up in a liberal family. You went to private school, I'm willing to bet on that. You can have anything you want.

SAMARA

My parents are completely opposed to my faith.

LAYLA

Have they kicked you out of the house? You do live at home, right? We're talking about women without any choices at all.

ANIS

In pre-revolutionary Iran, the Shah's secret police tore veils off with swords.

LAYLA

Ok, fine. And then the mullahs forced them to put them back on.

SANIYA

You really want to live in Saudi Arabia? They're not going to let you be a writer there.

SAMARA

I respect what you're saying. But my faith isn't a trend.

LAYLA

Come on. You're smart, you're gorgeous, you're "hip." What the fuck are you doing here? And why do you keep coming back?

RAGAB.

RAGAB

Excuse me, ladies. Sorry to interrupt.

ANIS alone.

ANIS

(*to audience*) In downtown Cairo you can buy a designer burkha made by Chanel, with lingerie to match.

At my wedding, every woman wore the hijab.

SAMARA. Though we can't see him yet, she is talking to RAGAB. ANIS thinks she is talking to him.

SAMARA

Beautiful evening.

ANIS

Yeah. I was just looking at the stars.

She puts down her purse.

SAMARA

Can I talk to you for a moment?

ANIS

Uh …

RAGAB appears.

RAGAB

I'd love to. Come out on the balcony.

SAMARA

Great.

They go.

ANIS alone. He looks at the purse. Clears his throat.

ANIS

Um, hello? You forgot your purse.

Probably she wanted me to look in it. You know, subconsciously that's why she left it.

He opens the purse.

Takes out the BlackBerry.

Pretty cool. Needless to say they're not standard issue at the Egyptian Ministry of Health.

What I was hoping for? A gale force wind? To sweep away the tomb of dust? That had suffocated my heart?

He reads the BlackBerry.

RAGAB and SAMARA on the balcony.

RAGAB

I enjoyed our little coffee at the Hilton.

SAMARA

What about the waitresses? They were all slobbering over you.

RAGAB

Occupational hazard.

SAMARA

It that exciting for you?

RAGAB

Not so much anymore.

SAMARA

Why do you flirt with them then?

RAGAB

I am a man. It's why you're wearing that hijab, right? So I won't get tempted.

SAMARA

It's your life.

RAGAB

Sometimes it doesn't feel that way.

SAMARA

Nice. Good line.

RAGAB

I'm serious. It's strange, representing—I don't have your fancy words ... Movies mean a lot to people, that's all.

SAMARA

Just like my parents. No values, no belief in anything. Except big TVs and nice cars.

RAGAB

Just because you have a big TV doesn't mean you don't have any values. I just got a fifty-inch plasma real cheap in Kuwait.

Don't we always want to challenge our parents?

SAMARA

When they drive a BMW through huge slums, and refuse to look out the window, I don't know what they expect.

She looks for her BlackBerry.

RAGAB

What?

SAMARA

My BlackBerry. I must have left my purse inside.

RAGAB

Expecting a call?

SAMARA
This guy.

RAGAB
When you're young, it seems like everything can be
changed. As you get older, you start to realize—I'm not a
good talker but, you know, like Anis says, the world's
billions of years old.

SAMARA
You're not that old.

RAGAB
Thank you.

SAMARA
Somebody like you could make a big difference.

RAGAB
What do you mean?

SAMARA
If you took a stand.

RAGAB
Oh, I see.

SAMARA
Something simple. Like if you came out and said you
thought we should have free elections. Just as an opinion.

RAGAB
I'm not political, I'm an actor.

SAMARA
With enormous influence.

RAGAB

I'm not sure I want the extremists running this joint.

SAMARA

What do you mean? You people are always talking about extremists, and Islamists; those are words made up by the *New York Times*. We're so brainwashed, we even say the Middle East. East of what? London and New York? What if we're not the East. What if we're the centre.

RAGAB

What about that guy, at *The Faith*? Sheikh Ahmad.

SAMARA

Sheikh Ahmad. Yeah. I just found out something pretty interesting about Sheikh Ahmad.

RAGAB

I don't even really know who he is.

SAMARA

What about our government? Three billion dollars a year buys the Americans unlimited access to our torture chambers, no questions asked.

People look up to you. You're a role model.

RAGAB

Nobody elected me.

SAMARA

Nobody elected our government either.

RAGAB

That's why I just try to be myself.

SAMARA

Except when hot waitresses throw themselves at you.

He kisses her. The whale rises.

RAGAB
Well, that was kind of like kissing Switzerland.

SAMARA
I'm not trying to seduce you.

RAGAB
OK, fine. You could have asked me to stop.

SAMARA
I want you to help.

RAGAB
That's cool.

SAMARA
It's important. Like not always thinking about yourself.

RAGAB
I got you.

SAMARA
I should go.

RAGAB
What's the hurry?

SAMARA
I've got a deadline.

RAGAB
I'll walk you out. It's late.

SAMARA
Thanks, I'm good.

RAGAB

Cool.

ANIS puts the BlackBerry down. The whale appears.

ANIS

Of course. Stupid me.

He crawls to the edge of the water.

AMM appears.

AMM

I just saw Saddam being hanged. Somebody recorded it on a cell phone. They pushed him and yelled taunts. Then the floor opened up and he fell. It reminded me of those beheadings Al-Qaeda used to broadcast from Iraq.

ANIS

Get me one of your street girls.

AMM

Why?

ANIS

I want to get laid. Go!

AMM

Astakh fur Allah.

AMM leaves.

ANIS

He reads from the BlackBerry.

She was writing an article. About us.

"Like so many of us, Anis Zaki has experienced painful loss. But because he refuses to face it, he has become a metaphor for everything that is wrong with our hijacked culture. After years of escape and addiction, what Zaki most clearly resembles is one of our ancient tombs, of the sort that tourists fly to Egypt to gawk at. Pry Mr. Zaki open and all you find is a disintegrating pile of bones."

I was research. We all were. A means to an end. A journalist is always at work.

The whale returns.

Hang tight. I'm coming very soon.

Five.

Party. Next one. A night or two later. All are there. Raucous.
ANIS is trying to make a speech. At first it's hard to get
everyone's attention.

ANIS
> Forgive me, I've prepared a speech. Think of me as
> Saddam if he hadn't been hanged before he could testify
> about who helped pay for all his crimes.

RAGAB
> Saddam who?

ANIS
> For many years we've been gathering on this houseboat.
> During which I, as you always remind me, haven't really
> said much.

MUSTAFA
> But your silence is like another man's *Magnum opus*, my
> boy.

ANIS
> Shut up.

MUSTAFA
> Just kidding.

ANIS

But things change, sometimes when you least expect them to. So now, I must speak. On the advice of a friend, you see, I went to a doctor.

SANIYA

A doctor. How did you get in?

ALI

He does work for the Ministry of Health.

ANIS

I said shut the fuck up.

SANIYA

He's frisky tonight.

ANIS

Frisky. This doctor, so-called, said that I was sick—I don't know how many years of medical school you need to diagnose that. Then he—or she, hard to tell which—prescribed some fresh air, and a visit to the Hilton Hotel. I said that with my back, in my condition, there was no chance of that.

MUSTAFA

It's full of rich ponces anyway.

ANIS

Should I wait until you're finished? Is the burden of listening just too great? Are you five years old?

LAYLA

Anis.

ANIS

Given that I can barely walk, and I certainly can't afford an army of overpriced antidepressants, and given the fact I'm even allowed on this boat is an act of charity that I should probably be ashamed of …

RAGAB

It's my pleasure, Anis.

ANIS

Given all that, and a few other things, I've decided that there's only one way for me to get better. And that, my friends, is to smear us all in that underrated salve called the truth.

ALI

The truth about what?

ANIS

Good. I wanted to start with you.

ALI

Bring it on.

ANIS

You know how we've all always wondered how Ali could possibly make a living running a little shit magazine that only about twelve people a week actually read? Well, he doesn't. He has another job. One he's kept a secret from us for a very long time.

SANIYA

That's not true.

ANIS

Yes, even from you, his concubine.

SANIYA
Actually, he's the concubine.

RAGAB
What is he, a truck driver?

ANIS
That's what's interesting.

LAYLA
No, I bet you sell something. It's the moustache.

SANIYA
What would he sell?

RAGAB
Teeth whitening strips.

MUSTAFA
No, Viagra.

LAYLA
Egyptian Viagra.

MUSTAFA
That's right! It prevents erections.

RAGAB
The whole army's on it.

LAYLA
That finally explains the '67 war.

MUSTAFA
And the '73 war.

RAGAB
And the '49 war.

LAYLA
Has Egypt ever won a war?

ANIS
Ah, funny funny funny.

You're all familiar with the publication *The Faith*, of course.
Compulsory reading for apocalyptic jihadists, I think Ali
called it.

Please, allow me to introduce you to Sheikh Ahmad.

ANIS indicates ALI.

LAYLA
No.

SANIYA
Don't be ridiculous.

ANIS
It's a—what do you call it—pen-name. Right, Ali?

Silence.

LAYLA
Oh my God.

MUSTAFA
Ahmad's a fucking lunatic!

ALI
Yeah, and?

LAYLA
He supports beheading!

MUSTAFA

You're a Christian.

ALI

So?

LAYLA

Ahmad said we should string up the infidels. You were
talking about yourself.

MUSTAFA

You called yourself the enemy within.

ALI

I have to eat. I got purged from the University, remember?
They cancelled my tenure.

LAYLA

Because you were a Christian!

ALI

I still am. I try, I mean the jihadist rhetoric is such a cliché,
really I'm almost writing parody.

LAYLA

Who the fuck's going to get that?

ALI

It's not like I believe it. At least not any more than you
believe your bullshit press releases. It's a gig. An easy gig.
I can do a thousand words in about seven-and-a-half
minutes. You think I make money running *Cairo Now*?

SANIYA

You're Sheikh Ahmad.

RAGAB

It's hilarious!

SANIYA
No, it's not.

ALI
Come on, baby. Some of us need to have jobs.

MUSTAFA
Peasants read that stuff, makes them think it's a good idea
to hack off somebody's head.

ALI
Give me a break. You deal toilets to the US Marines.

ANIS
Toilets? No, no. Not just toilets.

MUSTAFA
What are you talking about?

ANIS
The truth. In fact, that whole selling-latrines-to-the-US-
Army thing is just a small part of his little Third World
empire.

You see, our man Mustafa's pretty clever. Talk about the
latrines and the Americans, then no one will notice what
he's really up to.

MUSTAFA
And what is that?

ANIS
How many times you been to Israel in the last six months?
You see, certain Israelis want to buy up as much of the
West Bank as they can before some kind of peace treaty
gets imposed.

Trouble is, Palestinians can't sell their land to Israelis. It's
considered treason. Egyptians, on the other hand—well,

that's a different story. Easy enough for one of us to buy
land from a bunch of destitute farmers, then sell it to
whoever can pay the highest price, whether they're from
Brooklyn or Tel Aviv. Justice, peace, whatever. It's all
about buyers and sellers, right?

You tear down the olive groves personally, or do you hire
the farmers to do it to themselves?

MUSTAFA
Where'd you get this?

ANIS
I don't remember.

MUSTAFA
Fuck you. Who have you been talking to?

Everything I do is totally on the up and up. Completely
legal. I get permits. Whatever.

Wow. What a great night, everybody. Thanks so much.

LAYLA
Do you really?

MUSTAFA
What?

LAYLA
Buy Palestinian land and sell it to Israelis?

MUSTAFA
Do you really?

LAYLA
What?

MUSTAFA

Enjoy going down on your knees and begging Saniya for your rent?

ALI

OK, that's enough.

RAGAB

Relax. He's high. Blowing off steam.

MUSTAFA

Yeah. And I'm gone.

Pause.

ANIS

Was it something I said?

SANIYA

We try to be kind. We try to take care of you.

ANIS

How much does your charming husband make driving destitue peasants out of their shacks in the Old City? I always wanted to know. Now, I do. Two-and-a-half million pounds in 03–04, if my research is correct, which I'm betting that it is.

"Slumlord" is the word, isn't it? Remember in school, when you always used to talk about "helping" the poor?

LAYLA

Fuck you.

SANIYA and LAYLA storm out. ALI follows.

ALI

Asshole.

ALI follows.

ANIS

What a cheeky sheikhy. I don't know, Samara. The truth hurts.

RAGAB

Holy shit, Anis.

AMM enters.

AMM

The police have just arrested twenty-three Islamic extremists. Say they were plotting to blow up the Mogamma Building. That's where you work, isn't it?

ANIS

They'd be doing me a favour.

RAGAB

What about me? Aren't you going to have a go at me?

ANIS

No.

RAGAB

Why not?

ANIS moves toward the water.

Anis! God, what are you doing?

ANIS

Let me go.

RAGAB

Stop it. Amm! He's wasted. Put him to bed.

ANIS

It's her. It's all a big front. She's writing about us.

Pause. He looks at SAMARA. A beat.

RAGAB

We should go. I'll take you to Tahrir Square.

SAMARA

Thank you.

They leave. AMM puts him to bed.

AMM

Shhh. Lie down.

ANIS

The boat. There's waves. It's moving. I can feel it.

AMM

The boat's fine. You never told them what happened to your wife and daughter.

ANIS

No.

AMM

Why not?

ANIS

Help!

AMM

What?

ANIS

I'm being swallowed.

I remember, the night of my wedding. The smell of the orange blossoms. Oh, they were in full bloom.

Adila.

That was my wife's name.

Six.

Later. SAMARA returns. She looks around.

SAMARA
Hey. Wake up.

ANIS
Huh?

SAMARA
My stuff. My BlackBerry. Please.

ANIS
What time is it? God, I feel sober.

SAMARA
My purse.

ANIS
Who's the article for? *The Faith*?

SAMARA
They came to me.

ANIS
A commission. Of course. Sell, baby. Sell sell sell.

SAMARA
I wasn't going to use your names.

ANIS

Just the "movie star." But then he's the exception, the ray of light in the murky den of vice. The one you can turn around. I love that—how, in your article, you expect he'll be the worst, and then he ends up being the one who can change.

SAMARA

At least he's willing to listen. It's a big world out there. While you sit around and get baked, things are happening.

ANIS

Like an Islamic revolution.

SAMARA

You prefer a dictatorship?

ANIS

I prefer getting high.

SAMARA

I don't think anybody could stop you from doing that.

ANIS

Ha.

SAMARA

Look, I'm sorry. Being secretive is part of my job. Now can I please have my stuff?

ANIS

Let's play a game. That's what you like, right—games? It's in this room somewhere. You look for it, and I'll tell you whether you're close or not.

SAMARA stares at him.

Oh, forget it.

He gets the purse.

You have about a hundred messages. Who's the persistent guy?

SAMARA
Who says I'm even planning to submit the story?

ANIS
I say ten days.

SAMARA
Until what?

ANIS
Ragab dumps you. That's longer than most, because you're pretty formidable—I'll give you that. But I highly advise you to keep stringing him along. Once he's tasted conquest, he gets bored real fast. Mr. Cut and Run.

SAMARA
That's great. Of course you assume I'm in love with him.

ANIS
Aren't you?

SAMARA
Just because he's a good-looking movie star.

ANIS
If you prefer ugly and anonymous, I'm right here.

SAMARA
You've already revealed your taste. You only like the pipe. Did you read my notes about you?

ANIS
    I did.

SAMARA
    Super nice guy, smart, obviously well-read. Dig deep
    though—

ANIS
    I remember. Just a disintegrating pile of bones.

SAMARA
    Lots of people have grief, you know. This whole world is
    full of grief. So what? How many dead children and
    mothers every day in Iraq? In the territories? Here? In
    EGYPT? Why do you get to sit around and dwell on your
    tragedy? It's real, I know, painful, I know—but what
    makes it so special? When I was born, there were forty
    million people in this country. Now there's eighty, and
    while you all sit around getting stoned, most of them have
    to buy filthy water from trucks.

ANIS
    Let them eat BlackBerry. Not the fruit, the handheld
    device. Remember? Coltan, in the Congo?

    *ANIS goes to the water. SAMARA follows him, with the
    BlackBerry.*

SAMARA
    Look.

    She presses a button.

Gone.

ANIS
    Congratulations.

SAMARA

Fuck you.

ANIS

Excuse me. I'm just going to go for a quick ride on the whale.

ANIS flies through the stars.

Seven.

At least a few days later. All but SAMARA and ALI. AMM stands in the room. Silence.

AMM
Happy Festival Day.

MUSTAFA
The ashtray.

   Pause.

Basically I went home, I looked myself in the mirror, and I said, "Mustafa, what the fuck are you doing? Fifty Palestinians die for every Israeli killed in that horrible war, and on top of it you sell off their land. Shouldn't the buck stop here?"

LAYLA
And?

MUSTAFA
The jury's still out.

   AMM spits.

I don't see you running away from the paycheque you squeeze out of us.

AMM
Happy Festival Day.

MUSTAFA
Fine. Happy Festival Day.

Pause.

ALI enters.

LAYLA crosses away from ALI.

ALI
What?

Pause.

RAGAB
Anis. You've gone all quiet again.

Pause.

SANIYA
That's what happens when your heart gets broken.

Pause.

MUSTAFA
Pass the pot. Anis. Pot.

ANIS
It's gone.

MUSTAFA
What do you mean it's gone?

ANIS
I smoked it all.

AMM
Festival Day. When the Prophet, peace be upon him, led
the unbelievers to Mecca.

SAMARA.

Long pause.

RAGAB
Samara.

SAMARA
Hello.

Silence. MUSTAFA makes a whale noise.

MUSTAFA
Oh my God, Anis. Look, it's your whale.

RAGAB
Shh.

This is a surprise.

A whale noise.

A good surprise.

Silence.

Another whale noise.

Stop it.

SAMARA
You told them.

RAGAB
Yes.

SAMARA
I owe you an apology.

After I first came, I just mentioned that I'd been here, in passing. To Abdullah Hussein, the editor of *The Faith*. It was his idea. I didn't want to write it. Or, I did at first, but then …

RAGAB
We understand. These things happen.

SAMARA
I told them I wouldn't publish it. I'll never work there again, if that means anything to you.

RAGAB
It does, actually. Right? Right?

ALI
Yeah.

SAMARA
(to ANIS) Hey. How are you?

ANIS
Great.

>*MUSTAFA clicks like a whale.*

MUSTAFA
That's a humpback. I did a little research.

>*AMM enters, on a mission to get ANIS. Sees SAMARA, happy that she's there.*

AMM
Happy Festival Day.

SAMARA
Happy Festival Day.

MUSTAFA
Get us some pot.

AMM
My dealer's dry. Police are all over the Old City.

MUSTAFA
Oh come on.

AMM
The extremists have ruined it for everybody.

*AMM signals to ANIS (he points to ANIS' crotch and gives the
equivalent to a thumbs up).*

RAGAB
OK, enough. Let's get out of here. It's Festival Day, we
need to have some fun. Come on, everybody up. Let's go
somewhere.

SANIYA
No thanks.

RAGAB
Aw, c'mon. Let's put all this shit behind us. We're
civilized. We know how to move on.

I know. Saqqara. The pyramids. At night, it's fantastic.
Seriously. There's these hidden passages. They're off-limits
to everybody. Nobody's allowed into these things. Not
even the tourists. But I know how to get in. We shot all the
alien scenes from *Scarab* there.

Come on, Mustafa, up.

MUSTAFA
Please don't touch me.

RAGAB
We'll stop and get some more dope. Omar's place is on the
way. He's got a huge stash.

MUSTAFA
Really?

RAGAB

Oh yeah. The guy is stoned 24/7.

MUSTAFA

Hey, Amm! You hear that? Omar Sharif's not having any
trouble getting pot!

A pot flies in.

MUSTAFA

So's your mama!

RAGAB

Up and at 'em! I've got my Escalade. Cadillac. Picked it up
in Bahrain. Roomy as hell, and pretty fast.

SAMARA

I'm into it.

LAYLA

Have fun.

SANIYA

Off you go.

RAGAB

Come on! Anis, you too.

ANIS

No.

RAGAB

Oh no. We're not going without the Master of Ceremonies.
You're not going to sit around here and feel sorry for
yourself. Come on people, time to let this shit go!

He goes to pick ANIS up.

ANIS

Get your hands off me.

RAGAB

Think of it as an intervention. Ready—one, two, three!

Eight.

At Saqqara. ALI, SANIYA, MUSTAFA and LAYLA at a lookout.

SANIYA
Well, this is awfully nice.

Where's Anis?

ALI
They're still in the car.

LAYLA
The tombs of our Pharaonic Forefathers.

MUSTAFA
Haven't been here in a dog's age, eh, Shake'n Bake?

SANIYA
Sheikh Ahmad. My God. You did quit, right? That isn't
another lie?

ALI
Yes, I quit.

LAYLA
Good.

SANIYA
How are you going to support yourself?

ALI

    I've taken a gig with *Middle East Bride*.

SANIYA

    Oh, dear.

ALI

    For once, being a Christian was an advantage.

LAYLA

    My boss told the President's office that he wrote my speech. They gave him a raise.

MUSTAFA

    Look at all the smog over the city.

ALI

    That statue's Horemheb.

LAYLA

    Tutankhamen's general. In grade six I got an A on the generals. Remember how they used to drag us here when we were in school?

MUSTAFA

    Right over by that sarcophagus is where I tried to kiss Mona Khatam.

LAYLA

    Got all hot and dusty looking at a bunch of old statues.

SANIYA

    Didn't understand it then. All this history.

LAYLA

    Our ancestors. Hard to believe, eh? The world's greatest ancient civilization.

ALI

We Christians are the real descendants of the Pharaohs.

MUSTAFA

You Christians are the real descendants of a couple of horny goats.

ALI

Them, and Adam and Eve. It was an ugly scene.

SANIYA

You know what? When we get back, I'm going to introduce you to my kids.

ALI

What?

SANIYA

Why shouldn't I? Why shouldn't my children meet the man I truly love?

ALI

Sweetheart.

SANIYA

Karim just got his first pimple. I've loved you since I was only a few years older than him.

MUSTAFA

Or you could make some little Christians of your own.

ALI

That's good too.

MUSTAFA

Hang on. I think I hear a biological clock. Is that you, Layla?

LAYLA

Tick tick tick.

Meanwhile, back at the car ... SAMARA and RAGAB up front, ANIS in the back, seemingly asleep. RAGAB is checking ANIS. RAGAB nods, ANIS is asleep.

RAGAB

Beautiful evening.

SAMARA

Yes. Can we get out of the car?

RAGAB

Sure.

You phoned me a couple of days ago. Call display.

SAMARA

Yeah.

RAGAB

You didn't leave a message.

SAMARA

I wasn't sure what to say.

RAGAB

"Hello" is good. "How's it going?"

I've been thinking about what you said. About me having a lot of influence. And the responsibility to do something positive with it.

SAMARA

Right.

RAGAB

Seriously. Even if it has a negative effect on my "career" or whatever. I mean, I've got it pretty good. If I can't take a risk, who can? Maybe I could make some kind of statement. Call a press conference. Nothing radical, but, you know, say I think we should have real elections.

SAMARA

That's great.

RAGAB

Great?

SAMARA

My dad told me that if I won't agree to marry his guy, he'll pull the plug.

RAGAB

Pull the plug?

SAMARA

Cut me off. Kick me out of the house. I don't make much money. I need their help.

RAGAB

That's tough.

SAMARA

I talked to my mom, but she won't do anything. Fuck. When it gets down to it, all they actually care about is being able to tell their friends that I'm married.

   Pause.

But if there was someone else.

RAGAB

Someone else?

SAMARA
Someone with potential.

RAGAB
Potential?

SAMARA
Yes. Down the road.

Pause.

RAGAB
That would be a huge step. For some.

SAMARA
Right.

RAGAB
It's a big commitment.

Pause.

You'd have to find the right … kind of person.

SAMARA
Yes.

RAGAB
Not that it's impossible, it's just …
People don't change overnight.

SAMARA
Sometimes people are taken by surprise.

RAGAB
Some people never change at all.
You'd need, you know, a very clear understanding.

SAMARA

Might not be necessary.

RAGAB

An arrangement. You know, one that allowed for—
autonomy, or freedom.

SAMARA

Freedom?

RAGAB

To be who we are.

SAMARA

And who are you?

RAGAB

Some guy who's always had a ton of luck. A selfish prick
who's met a girl that makes him think. Someone who
wants to figure out a way to give something back.

How about you? Who are you?

SAMARA

The daughter of parents who can't remember where they
came from. A woman. A Muslim. From the centre, not the
Middle East.

She kisses him. Touches her hair.

I guess it depends how you define it.

RAGAB

What?

SAMARA

Freedom.

RAGAB

Trouble is, everybody seems to define it their own way.

ANIS

It's hard to sleep when you're watching a romantic comedy. Not to mention a striptease.

RAGAB

I thought you were asleep.

ANIS

I want to go home.

RAGAB

We have to wait for Layla and them.

ANIS

We could try to commit suicide.

RAGAB

Come on, Anis.

The others return.

ALI

We could easily have been killed out there.

LAYLA

Oh my God, he ran away!

ALI

I told you. I saw some sort of animal. Looked like a large cat.

RAGAB

Your mood has improved.

SANIYA

Aren't you supposed to protect me from predators?

ALI

Cut and run, baby. Cut and run.

RAGAB

What were you guys doing?

ALI

We went for a lovely walk.

RAGAB

That's it?

ALI

No.

LAYLA

We fucked like monkeys on the Tomb of Horemheb.

RAGAB

Woo-hoo! I mean, oh.

MUSTAFA

Uh-oh, someone's turning into a prude. I wonder why.

SANIYA

You didn't find that offensive, did you, Samara?

SAMARA

No. It's fine.

RAGAB

Nice.

MUSTAFA

Good, because that wasn't offensive. What Mohammed did with pigs, now that's offensive.

LAYLA

Mustafa!

SAMARA

I beg your pardon?

SANIYA

That's right. You have to be fair, Mustafa. Don't forget what the Virigin Mary did to that donkey.

RAGAB

All right, that's enough.

MUSTAFA

Good. 'Cause there's no way I'm going to tell you what Moses did with that lamb.

LAYLA

I'm telling you, what we did at those tombs, that was God's work.

RAGAB

Let's get out of here.

ALI

It's still early, we should go somewhere else.

RAGAB

Where do you want to go?

ALI

The West Bank, Jeeves. And don't spare the camels!

LAYLA

The West Bank? What about the borders? The
checkpoints?

ALI

To hell with the checkpoints.

MUSTAFA

We could deliver my latrines on the way. They'd give me a
medal of honour for that.

SANIYA

They'd give you a medal of shit.

SAMARA

At least it'd match your tie.

RAGAB

Yes!

MUSTAFA

Nice one.

ALI

How about Baghdad? Let's go remind the Yankees we've
been hanging around these parts for a few thousand years.

SANIYA

We better tie up Sheikh Ahmad, here, though. He might
decide to martyr himself.

LAYLA

Fuck those fundamentalists!

MUSTAFA

And the imperialists!

SAMARA

And the secularists!

ALI

Not to mention the Symbolists!

SANIYA

What are you talking about?

ALI

It was an art joke.

MUSTAFA

It's their fault, all those fuckhead fucking fuck fucks! They bring us down, MAN!

LAYLA

Baghdad's only 700 clicks. We could be there by dawn.

MUSTAFA

Let's go to New York.

LAYLA

I've always wanted to go to New York.

ALI

This thing has wings on it, right?

RAGAB

Absolutely.

LAYLA

Take it up, Ragab.

(*sings*) I want to be a part of it ...

ANIS with the audience.

ANIS

You can probably see what's coming. I certainly did. A violent thump, and then the screeching of brakes. A long, silent pause, and then nervous, frightened talk. "Was that a body?" "No." "Yes." "A man." "Oh my God."

And then an argument, about what we should do, and if he could still be …

And then the revving of the engine and driving, fast, but careful, now, and more argument, Samara saying, "We should go back. We have to go back."

And then silence. And the whirr of the highway at night.

I didn't say a word. Because what I felt—unforgivably—was relief.

I was up all night, thinking about the person we hit. Then I fell asleep and I dreamt, of my wife and child, of the day it happened, of the phone call, and the way my throat seized when they told me. In my dream, I tried to remember that we all die, and that the path to heaven might be bordered by evergreens. And then Adila came to me. She said, "I am your wife." She touched my face and asked me, "What do you want?" And I said, "Some water, rain, a downpour." And she smiled and said, "You live on a houseboat. There is a world of water under your feet."

I woke up late. I walked to work. They fired me on the spot. And revoked my pension. And I was relieved.

AMM, next to him.

AMM

What happened?

ANIS looks at him.

Are you OK?

ANIS

Never been better, Amm. Never been better.

AMM watches him.

107

Nine.

The others step out of the car. They join him. It is the next night.
SAMARA has a newspaper.

Long pause.

ANIS
How's everybody doing? My back kills.

LAYLA
Shush.

ANIS
Oh, it's like that, is it?

Pause. AMM enters.

AMM
A man in his forties was killed on the road to Saqqara last
night. Hit by a speeding car. Massive trauma to his head,
neck and spine. No one has come to claim the body. Police
are appealing for information from anyone who may have
seen the unidentified man walking on the deserted stretch
of road.

Pause.

Just thought you might want to know.

AMM leaves.

MUSTAFA
Legally, we're fucked. It's textbook hit-and-run. Ten to fifteen years. More, if they send us to religious court.

LAYLA
It was an accident.

SANIYA
Can we not go over this again?

SAMARA
I told you to stop.

RAGAB
I ... I wasn't thinking.

ANIS
You refused to go back.

RAGAB
I was in shock.

SANIYA
I think we need to take care of each other right now.

ALI
That's right.

SANIYA
We're going to have to live with this for the rest of our lives. That's a lot.

ANIS
Compared to what? Getting smacked by a speeding Escalade?

RAGAB
  Light the pipe.

SAMARA
  You're going to smoke?

RAGAB
  Looks that way.
  Sorry.

ANIS
  There's no dope.
  Been years since I went this long. Almost twenty-four hours. Actually feels pretty good. I mean, not good, obviously, but all things considered.

LAYLA
  Shut up.

ANIS
  Of course. Shut up.

SAMARA
  We don't have any choice. We have to go to the police.
    Long pause.

RAGAB
  What?

SAMARA
  It's the right thing—

RAGAB
  It was an—

SAMARA
I know.

RAGAB
It'll be me—

SAMARA
I know.

RAGAB
But I thought we had agreed.

SAMARA
I didn't agree to anything. I was up all night.

LAYLA
We were all up all night.

ANIS
Amen to that.

MUSTAFA
Nobody's going to the police. There's other options. We just have to figure out who the man was, where he came from. Locate his relatives.

LAYLA
That's got to be simple enough.

MUSTAFA
Absolutely. And if he doesn't have any, well, we're off the hook. Once we've tracked them down, it's pretty simple. We offer to make a contribution. A significant contribution, right Ragab?

RAGAB
OK.

MUSTAFA
Compensation. Happens all the time. You make a mistake, you pay for it. That's all.

LAYLA
American army did it. Remember? With that fifteen-year-old those marines raped in Alexandria.

MUSTAFA
And that was no accident.

SANIYA
Nobody has to know where the money came from.

MUSTAFA
Yeah yeah—a proxy. You run it through a business. Or a charity. Easy. Boom boom boom.

RAGAB
Because it was an accident.

SAMARA
But you wouldn't go back. He could have been alive, for hours. That's all I could see, all night. This man, on the road, torn apart, bleeding. What if he was still conscious? What if he lay there all night?

RAGAB
We hit him hard. I don't think there's any chance he could have survived.

LAYLA
I'm not going to jeopardize my fucking job.

SAMARA
I'm trying not to think about myself.

ALI

I think it's important to put this in perspective.

ANIS

Perspective?

ALI

People die every day. All over the world—dead from war,
dead from terrorism, from no food, from Islamists and
Israelis and Westerners and goddamn weather. And
nobody has to go to jail.

ANIS

Not if they run away.

ALI

What's the point in going to the police? It's not going to
bring the man back to life. You're right—we were idiots.
Driving stoned, fast, idiots. Selfish fucks. And rude to you,
too. But I know what it's like to be sacrificed, Samara.
When they purged all the Christians at the University,
suddenly I had nothing. I had to start all over again.
There's nothing noble about that. It's just fucking hard.

MUSTAFA

And you didn't have to go to jail.

ALI

I was lucky.

MUSTAFA

I've spent a bit of time in our country's fine prison system.
Pious isn't the word that comes to mind.

ALI

You keep going forward, one foot in front of the other.
That's all anybody does. Why make it any more impossible
than it already is?

SANIYA produces a substantial amount of money.

SANIYA

It took a while, but I got it. I snuck into the house and tore
up his bedroom. It was in the mattress. Big stash.
Sonofabitch is going to kill me. But who cares.

She goes to LAYLA.

First, for you.

LAYLA

No, no.

SANIYA

Take it. Really. I'm sorry I always make you beg.

LAYLA

Thanks.

SANIYA

You're welcome.

She produces more money.

This is for the man's family. I trust you'll get it to him.

MUSTAFA

Damn straight.

SANIYA goes to SAMARA.

SANIYA

I've been hard on you. And I'll admit it's because I was—
am—jealous. Jealous of your youth, of how you're what
the world is becoming. What's the point in punishing the

114

past? Better to look to the future, don't you think? All of
our futures.

SAMARA

I wouldn't know how to live with myself.

MUSTAFA

You'll figure it out.

ALI

It's part of getting older.

SANIYA

You're not the first to fall in love with him, you know.
We've all fallen in love with him. Even the men, though
they don't like to admit it.

But you're the first to change him. Really. For weeks, no
young thing on his arm, no running off to something more
important. Caring about the world. Politics. It's amazing.

It's funny, now I can almost imagine him settling down,
maybe even having children.

Ragab? Don't you think?

Pause.

RAGAB

Yeah. I do.

Pause. SAMARA looks at RAGAB.

RAGAB goes to her.

ANIS

Oh no. Not you too. Please, not you. Thirteen hours ago
we KILLED A MAN.

SANIYA

Anis.

AMM enters with a small package, pleased with himself.

AMM
Finally. I sweat and blood and tears to get them.

MUSTAFA goes to get it.

MUSTAFA
Nice work, Nubia-boy.

AMM
They're for Anis.

ANIS
Let him have it.

MUSTAFA
Great. Let's fire this puppy up.

MUSTAFA takes the package. Fills the pipe.

AMM
What are you doing? That's not dope. It's the herbs.

ANIS
Just go!

AMM
Arabs.

AMM leaves.

MUSTAFA
Give me the lighter. I want to get blotto.

ANIS
Too bad.

MUSTAFA
  What?

ANIS
  How it evaporates.

SAMARA
  What?

ANIS
  Conviction. Principle. Maybe it's because he saw your
  hair.

  Do I get an invite to the wedding? Amazing. You'd feel
  bad for what, a day a week, and then you'd filter back and
  it'd all be like nothing ever changed.

  MUSTAFA lights the herbs.

  Like nothing ever changes. God damn it, something's
  going to change!

  MUSTAFA coughs.

MUSTAFA
  Ah. Amm, you trying to poison us? What the hell is wrong
  with this dope?

AMM
  (*off*) It's not dope, you moron. It's the herbs!

  ANIS stands.

RAGAB
  That's enough, Anis.

ANIS
  Don't get all negative. Whoa, standing is so painful.
  Excuse me.

  RAGAB blocks his exit.

ANIS
Just try to run with this for a bit.

RAGAB
Where are you going?

ANIS
About four-and-a-half blocks from here. To the police
station on Gemayel Avenue. Given the state of my back,
it'll take me at least half an hour, if not more. So if you're
planning on hiding out, I suggest you make your break
very soon.

SANIYA
Anis, it's all over. We've agreed.

ANIS
I haven't agreed. I've never agreed.

MUSTAFA
I feel sick.

ANIS
Think of me as Jonah. Imagine I've been saved by the
whale.

RAGAB
You're a fucking nut!

   He lunges for ANIS.

LAYLA
Ragab!

ALI
Enough!

ANIS
Don't you touch—

SANIYA
You'll just make it worse.

RAGAB
I'm not—

ANIS
Don't touch me!

RAGAB
I'm not touching him!

ANIS
Get your hands off me!

MUSTAFA
Oh, my God.

ALI
Ragab, easy.

RAGAB
What am I supposed to do? It's me that's going to take the fall!

SANIYA
He's going through withdrawal.

LAYLA
Here, have a puff.

MUSTAFA
No, don't.

ANIS
This is the best thing that's happened in so long.

ALI
Just sit there, and don't move.

RAGAB
We've been pussyfooting around it for too long. You're sick, and you need help. And if you just calm down a little, I'm going to help you get it.

ANIS lunges at him. RAGAB takes him down.

ANIS
Get off me!

RAGAB
I'm going to take you to my doctor. No waiting, no line-ups. You should see his office. Leather couches, the whole bit. But you have to calm down.

RAGAB loosens his grip.

Samara told me, Anis. About your wife, about what happened before you came to Cairo. That's awful, horrible.

ANIS
I'll defend myself. It's my living right.

He goes in the back.

SAMARA
He got fired, they took away his pension.

ALI
What happened before he came to Cairo?

SANIYA
Anis, we'll help.

LAYLA
You can get another job.

ALI
I'll find you another job.

ANIS returns with a knife.

ANIS
I don't want a fucking job.

SANIYA
Anis, nobody's attacking you.

ANIS
(*to RAGAB*) I'm not one of your little whores.

RAGAB
Enough!

ANIS
It's good, don't you see? It's the water, the flood, the
answer to my goddamn prayers!

RAGAB
You're the one that buys whores!

LAYLA
Get the fuck out of here.

SANIYA
We'll deal with it. Wait outside.

RAGAB
And you can't even get it up!

SANIYA
Just go!

Cell. RAGAB pulls it out.

RAGAB

Hello? Hey, how's it going? Sorry, I got your message, it's just been crazy. No, no, it's a good time. Hang on a sec.

RAGAB goes.

MUSTAFA has a giant erection.

MUSTAFA

Me, too. This dope. I've got to …

LAYLA

What's wrong?

MUSTAFA

I'll meet you outside.

MUSTAFA goes.

ANIS

Samara wanted to stop. The rest of you were crazy, laughing.

SAMARA

Anis. It's over.

ANIS

I saw. She did, too. We knew what was coming.

SAMARA

How could you have known?

ANIS

Because it happened before, to little Hanni, and my wife, walking on the side of the road.

Pause.

SANIYA
Hanni?

LAYLA
His daughter.

SANIYA
How do you know?

LAYLA
He was in love with me once, too.

SAMARA goes to him.

SAMARA
It's going to be OK.

ANIS
No.

SAMARA
Sshhh.

ANIS
It'll just be the same as before.

SAMARA looks at them. SANIYA gestures to ALI and LAYLA.

ALI
I'll wait with you.

SANIYA
I need to go home.

LAYLA, SANIYA, ALI and MUSTAFA leave.

ANIS
I feel sick.

AMM enters.

AMM

What was he thinking?

ANIS

Who?

AMM

The asshole. He smoked the Sudanese herbs. I'm surprised they worked so well. Frankly, I thought they were a scam.

You were visited by the devil tonight.

AMM hands him a lit pipe.

Here. It's my personal stash.

ANIS

Thanks.

AMM leaves. ANIS smokes.

That's better. Hard thing, I'd imagine—if one is a believer, or trying to be one, anyway—is what to do now.

SAMARA

You're right. I should go to the police.

ANIS

I have a suggestion. Since you can't really do anything to help the dead man, you could try helping the half-dead one instead. You know, the one that the tourists gawk at. The pile of bones in the tomb.

SAMARA

How would I do that?

ANIS

You could try loving me back.

Pause.

Adila was always devout. Our marriage was arranged. Just before we were supposed to get married she started to get all political. I was like, "OK, you won't let me kiss you until after we're married and now you have to make an enemy of every powerful man in the village." The guy who bought and sold our cotton was a real chauvinist. Of course he was terrified of her, so he took it out on me.

I look at you and all I see is her.

SAMARA
But I'm not.

ANIS
I know.

She returns his book.

SAMARA
I'm no Prophet's daughter, either.

ANIS
Who are you, then?

SAMARA
Right now, I have no idea.

ANIS
You love Ragab.

SAMARA
That's an awful question.

ANIS
He's a good guy. That's what's so ...

SAMARA
I've got to go. I'm going to go to your office. And demand that they reinstate your pension.

OK? OK?

Pause. She turns to leave.

ANIS
Thank you.

SAMARA
You're welcome.

ANIS
That's what I was supposed to say, right?

SAMARA
I guess. I'm sorry.

ANIS
Me, too. Goodbye ...

She leaves.

(*sings softly*) ... farewell, auf Wiedersehen, goodnight.

AMM
NASA's found evidence of life on Mars. Pools of frozen water. They say once the climate was just like Earth's. And they've announced compensation for the Nubians. Because of the Aswan Dam. They've apologized for flooding our land. I'll get five thousand pounds.

Means I won't have to clean up around here anymore.

ANIS
Congratulations. That's good news.

AMM
Thank you.

It's time for the dawn prayer.

He leaves.

A cell. Obnoxious ring tone. Continues.

ANIS

Somebody had forgotten their cell.

I thought about answering it, about who it might be. Layla's boss, Ragab's agent, Samara's suitor ... maybe even the police.

He tokes. Ringing continues.

Then I started to wonder if it could be the man we killed, and if it was, who he might have been, and what he might want to say to us. I had an image in my head: a peasant, a villager, a father, eking out a living on the stinking trash heaps on the edge of the city. But then I realized that if it weren't for the generosity of my friends, the image I had in my head was really just a picture of me.

And then I was onto the Coltan and those children in the Congo, who never sleep because every night they have to walk miles to get away from their villages, so they won't be kidnapped by soldiers in their sleep. And me, and how easy I've got it, and that made me think about you. And what you think of when somebody says Egypt, the Middle East. And whether you should know or care that Persians and Arabs are not the same, that the nation of Iraq was created by the British in the 1920s, that there are highways in the West Bank reserved for Jews alone, and that in Egypt, like in a lot of places, some people get treated like slaves.

How about this. How about you just think about me. Little old me. Getting really stoned.

He smokes.

Lights fade.